FIRST GRADE
NOTEBOOK

BLANK + PRIMARY LINED NOTEBOOK
FOR DRAWING & WRITING

SUGGESTED USE:

TRY USING THE DOT GRID PAPER SECTION TO WRITE DOWN THE CHILD'S WORDS OR DESCRIPTIONS OF THEIR DRAWINGS IN MORE DETAIL THAN THEY COULD WRITE ON THEIR OWN, OR USE IT FOR TAPING IN PARTS OF WORKSHEETS ETC, AND THE BLANK AND LINED AREA CAN BE USED FOR THEM TO DRAW AND WRITE.

schoolnest

ART + BOOKS + NATURE

COPYRIGHT © 2023 BY MEGAN VAN SIPE

ALL RIGHTS RESERVED. NO PART OF THIS BOOK MAY BE REPRODUCED OR USED IN ANY MANNER WITHOUT WRITTEN PERMISSION OF THE COPYRIGHT OWNER.

SECOND EDITION

WWW.THESCHOOLNEST.COM

/   /

/   /

/   /

/   /

/ /

/   /

/   /

/   /

/ /

/   /

/   /

/   /

/   /

/ /

/ /

/   /

/   /

/ /

/   /

/   /

Thank you

FOR PURCHASING A SCHOOLNEST NOTEBOOK!

YOU CAN FIND A RAINBOW OF NOTEBOOK OPTIONS IN MANY SCHOOL SUBJECTS (MATH, SPELLING, HISTORY TIMELINE, SCIENCE, GRADE LEVEL COMPOSITION BOOKS, JOURNALS, AND MORE) ON:

<u>THESCHOOLNEST.COM</u>!

FOLLOW ALONG ON INSTAGRAM @SCHOOLNEST

Printed in France by Amazon
Brétigny-sur-Orge, FR

20636049R00114